S0-BFF-069

Squirrels and Chipmunks

By Allan Fowler

Consultants

Linda Cornwell, Learning Resource Consultant,
Indiana Department of Education

Fay Robinson, Child Development Specialist

Lynne Kepler, Educational Consultant

Children's Press®
A Division of Grolier Publishing
New York   London   Hong Kong   Sydney
Danbury, Connecticut

Project Editor: Downing Publishing Services
Designer: Herman Adler Design Group
Photo Researcher: Caroline Anderson

Library of Congress Cataloging-in-Publication Data

Fowler, Allan.
    Squirrels and chipmunks / by Allan Fowler.
      p. cm. – (Rookie read-about science)
    Includes index.
    Summary: Introduces members of the squirrel family, including
woodchucks and prairie dogs.
    ISBN 0-516-20323-1 (lib.bdg.)   0-516-26158-4 (pbk.)
    1. Squirrels—Juvenile literature. 2. Chipmunks—Juvenile literature.
[l. Squirrels.] I. Title. II. Series
    QL737.R68F68   1997   96-28769
    599.32'32–dc20   CIP
                                            AC

©1997 Children's Press®, a Division of Grolier Publishing Co., Inc.
All rights reserved. Published simultaneously in Canada.
Printed in the United States of America.
  2 3 4 5 6 7 8 9 10 R 06 05 04 03 02 01 00

Parks are for people.
But people are happy
to share many of their
parks with squirrels.

It's fun to watch
squirrels scampering
busily, their long, bushy
tails carried high.

In the fall, you might see squirrels gathering food and storing it away, so there will be enough to eat during winter.

People like to feed squirrels.

But a squirrel could bite
you, even if it's not on
purpose — so don't try
to put food right in a
squirrel's mouth.

Squirrels belong to
a family of mammals
called rodents.

It's quite a varied
family — mice, beavers,
and porcupines are
also rodents.

mouse

porcupine

9

The squirrels you most
often meet in parks are
gray squirrels.

You also see black squirrels in some places. They are the same animal as gray squirrels, except for their color.

Gray squirrels are one of many types of tree squirrels. They climb trees easily, and run along the branches.

They make their nests where
branches come together, or
in hollow tree trunks.

fox squirrel

flying squirrel

14

There are other kinds of tree squirrels, such as red squirrels, fox squirrels, and flying squirrels.

No, they don't really fly like birds.

A flying squirrel has a flap of skin on each side of its body, between its legs.

This skin helps it glide through the air, from branch to branch.

Ground squirrels don't live in trees, but on the ground — or in it. They may dig holes, called burrows, and nest there.

ground squirrel

red squirrel

Most kinds of ground squirrels hibernate. That means they go into a long sleep during winter. Tree squirrels do not hibernate.

If you like to walk in the woods, you've probably seen chipmunks darting around.

A chipmunk is really a sort of ground squirrel.

You can recognize a chipmunk by its color — light or reddish brown with black and white stripes on its back and cheeks.

Chipmunks are smaller than most squirrels.

An adult chipmunk might be only five or six inches long, and weigh only a few ounces.

They have pouches in their cheeks for carrying food.

23

Squirrels and chipmunks
eat acorns and other nuts,
fruit and berries, seeds,
insects — and sometimes
eggs and even small birds.

Their four big front
teeth never get worn
down, because they keep
on growing.

prairie dogs

Some kinds of squirrels have tails that are shorter and less bushy than those of gray squirrels.

woodchuck

Woodchucks — also called groundhogs — and prairie dogs are members of the squirrel family.

The squirrel family is a big one. Squirrels of one kind or another live in most parts of the world.

So if you visit a faraway city, you might meet a squirrel or a chipmunk.

It would be like running into an old friend from home.

Words You Know

flying squirrel

fox squirrel

gray squirrel

red squirrel

beaver

chipmunk

mouse

porcupine

prairie dogs

woodchuck

31

Index

About the Author

Allan Fowler is a free-lance writer with a background in advertising.
Born in New York, he lives in Chicago now and enjoys traveling.

Photo Credits

©Ben Klaffke — 3, 6

Visuals Unlimited — ©John Gerlach, cover (background), 23; ©Gary W. Carter, 24 (background); ©S. Maslowski, 5, 13, 14, 17, 24 (inset), 30 (top left); ©W. J. Weber, 9 (top), 31 (middle left); ©Tom J. Ulrich, 9 (bottom), 31 (middle right), 11; ©Milton H. Tierney, Jr., 12; ©J. D. Cunningham, 10, 30 (bottom left); ©Leonard Lee Rue III, 14 (top), 30 (top right); ©Glenn M. Oliver, 18; ©George Herben, 19; ©Stephen J. Lang, 21, 31 (top right); ©Joe McDonald, 27, 29, 31 (bottom right)

Comstock — ©Comstock, 26, 31 (bottom left); ©Art Gingert, 4

Cover: Red squirrel